I0447674

Dogs, Water, Church and Black People ©

'A Timely Conversation'

Kirk Ray Smith Sr., BS, MS, ABD

Contributions from Robyn Mahaffey, BS, MA. Ed

Kirk Smith Unlimited

TABLE OF CONTENTS

Chapter One

A Case for the Conversation

I'm sure you may have thought to yourself after reading the title of this book, 'seriously, dogs, water, church and black people?' At least this is what I was thinking when the unction to write such a piece initially came over me. Although the title admittedly sounds ambiguous, sophomoric, and even somewhat offensive, the relationship between dogs, water, church and Black people is quite fascinating, from both historical and contemporary perspectives. This is particularly true here in the United States. As your mind begins to wonder even more, I would encourage you to allow your thoughts to take you where they may. As you travel intellectually through this piece, while you may or may not agree with its conclusions, you will be mentally stimulated and organically engage in an obscure, almost nonexistent conversation. The conclusions embedded in this moderately subjective paper are based on both anecdotal and existential experience, knowledge and observation. What makes me appear to be moderately subjective on this topic is that I happen to be a man of color, more specifically, a black man, a.k.a. African-American...pick one. Although there will be potentially multiple outcomes, the four objectives I have for this piece are to start a larger and/or three distinct simultaneous conversations and provoke thought around these topics, inspire others to count on history (use it as advantage/leverage for a better future) instead of discounting it (running away from it), address and illuminate three dimensions of the African-American experience, and finally, promote and galvanize unity by understanding and appreciating our differences.

Take just a moment. Close your eyes. Now, think about dogs: what you know, how you feel. What are some generalizations that you mentally make concerning dogs and black people? Without conducting any parse analysis or data collection, would you agree that more white individuals and families (by measure) are pet owners than black individuals and families within this country? Let's do the same with water. Think about how you feel. Think about what you see on TV. What observations can you make concerning water and black people? Again, without research, would you agree that swimming and water sports are a lot more popular (by measure) among whites than blacks in our nation? Lastly, with eyes closed, think about church? Is church, not simply religion, but the need for spiritual acceptance and hope? Does this seem to be a significant need in the black community? Before you close this book, delete it or throw it in the trash, before you close your mind if you decide to continue, humor me for a little while as I attempt to take you on a journey that will surely peak your interest on a thought provoking side of these issues.

Have you ever wondered where your personal phobias came from? We're we born with certain fears? What about voices in your head, we all have them. Sometimes these voices encourage us, and at other times they discourage and frustrate us. The best of us can easily think evil-dark thoughts, although most people never act on these thoughts, they're there nonetheless; no one is exempt nor above this reproach. I've often said, neurotics build castles in the sky, and psychotics move in. The fine line between thinking or feeling something and actually acting on it can be both fascinating and scary. Often times what hinders us or causes pause and pain, are things that happen in the past, whether we participated in or witnessed those things or not. These feelings can be caused by vivid memories or stories told to us about our family member's experiences from the past. The reality is there are things that have happened within our families before we were born that haunt us today. The once popular, not very friendly term trauma-echo comes to mind. According to many clinicians, trauma-echo is when people with histories of significant trauma find themselves repeating distressful behaviors despite a desire to recover. Many find themselves, for example, in abusive relationships later in life even though they were severely and adversely affected by abuse in the past. Living within these later relationships can cause a 'trauma echo' in which the feelings and behaviors associated with the original trauma 'echo' or recur throughout other relationships long after the original trauma has passed (Addiction.com, 2015). Thoughts and feelings from traumatic events can be passed down subconsciously through the generations. This creates a cycle that is not easily broken. This piece isn't anti-dog, anti-water, or anti-church by no stretch of the imagination. What it is unequivocally without trepidation or hesitation is pro-understanding, pro-unity and must be discussed TNT (today-not-tomorrow).

Chapter Two

Dogs: A Man's Best Friend or Maybe Not

Dogs: A Man's Best Friend or Maybe Not

Although I grew up with dogs in my home, I've always had an inexplicable fear of them. As a young boy, every time I heard a dog bark or saw a dog walking the streets or in someone's yard, fear would come over me out of nowhere. There wouldn't have had to be an imminent threat or implied threat, I just feared dogs. Again, I had a number of dogs throughout my childhood, but I simply tolerated having them around. There was no special bond or fondness for them at all. Dogs were not popular in the neighborhood I grew up in. With the exception of a few streets, the area was too urban for pets; too many apartment buildings, storefronts and 'concrete' for a dog or cat to be comfortable. There were no front lawns, backyards or parks for them to run around; I saw more dead dogs than living. I actually saw a dog dragged by a car once and thought nothing of it; just another dead animal to me. Before you judge and paint the entire black community with a broad-brush and start shaking your fist, hear me out and listen closely. I decided to ask around about different one's feelings about dogs as pets. These are two people from my inner circle. They grew up in African American communities but they weren't as urban as mine. It shocked me because I thought I was atypical in my feelings about dogs.

> *"There were not many families with dogs in our neighborhood. Ours and another house on the street both owned German Shepherds that were not really socialized. They didn't run up and down the street or play with the kids. When they did accidently get out, all the kids ran. Even me, and*

it was my dog! There was no love lost when my dad got rid of him."

"The dogs in our neighborhood walked around with the older boys on these ugly, monstrous collars and leashes. Everyone was afraid when they came by the park. The boys thought it was cool and wanted to walk around with scary dogs. The girls thought the boys were cute and thought nothing about the dogs."

There seems to be this expectation that in America, we're all supposed to love dogs in the same way we love people. We see images where it's acceptable to kiss dogs, let them lick our faces, eat off our plates and sleep in our beds alongside us. While this is cute, fun and normal to many, it's not cute, fun or expected by others. I love how people with dogs say 'he won't bite, he's a sweet dog'; really? You ever notice how the media is quick to show a person being injured, maimed, shot and even killed on national television over and over, but would never show a dog being injured, shot or ran over by a car. We rarely see a dog mauling or the effects after a person has been bitten or mauled. To my knowledge, dog attacks are not used as one of the many homicide cases on popular reality crime shows. According to Brandongaille.com and statista.com 22% of black families own dogs compared to 61% of white families. The numbers have fluctuated slightly over the years; however, the fact remains the same. Overall, (generally speaking) dogs are not a big deal to black folks. Is it that we, as African Americans dislike dogs? Whatever the case we have a different historical relationship with our four-legged friends than that of our white brothers and sisters.

Since the start of the American slave trade, dogs have been used as weapons to tame, maim, train, contain, scare and even kill black people. Let's take a brief look at how this trauma echo started for African-Americans. Without parse research, we can all agree that if a slave got out of line or attempted to escape dogs were used to attack them and/or hunt them down. We can also agree that before and during the Civil Rights movement dogs were trained and used by law enforcement to attack blacks on a consistent basis. Whether they were used to break up protests, peaceful gatherings or simply intimidate minorities, dogs were clearly communicated and understood as weapons to be feared. A moderate look at the type of dogs used against blacks during the fifties, sixties, and even the seventies, helps clarify reasons as to why African-Americans choose to own certain types of dogs. Among the 22% of African American households that have dogs as pets, there is a marked commonality between breeds owned. The top ten preferred dog breeds include "tough guy" dogs like the Rottweiler, Bulldog, Doberman and the #1 breed, the Pitbull. These dogs are typically feared because of their build and perceived ferociousness. On the top ten list also were Boxers and Labradors. These dogs are considered nice, family dogs. They are smart and usually good with children. Surprisingly to me, making the list are Yorkies, Boston Terriers, Pugs and Chihuahuas. These little dogs are not very intimidating. Could the choice of dog be directly related to the feelings about dogs that have been passed down consciously or subconsciously through the generations? Are the trauma echoes so strong that we, as a community, systematically choose dogs that either project a totally viscous image or a totally nonthreatening and docile image? I believe it's a resounding yes!

We still have people alive today that are a direct product who participated in the Civil Rights Movement. Our grandparents and great aunts and uncles either experienced first-hand or saw on TV what happened to protestors during the Movement. Thus creating and/or perpetuating the trauma echo. The Pitbull is a "Tough guy" dog that is considered to be the most popular breed of dog in the African American community. The dog is loved by many. It is also considered to be dangerous and unpredictable by many legislators. Currently there are approximately 25 states that have Breed-Specific-Bans on these dogs. In 2015, 82% of the fatal attacks by dogs were by Pitbulls. Since 1998 there have been 285 fatal Pitbull attacks. Why would we gravitate to the type of dog that has such a reputation? Trauma echoes have prompted African Americans with a sense of urgency to protect themselves. Whether it be by getting a good education, or moving to the suburbs, or something as simple as owning a dog with a "don't mess with me" reputation, African Americans are still whirling from the effects of slavery, Jim Crow and the Civil Rights Movement.

Pitbulls can be wonderful pets when trained and loved, just like any other breed. Many African-American households that own dogs, love their pets very much. They even consider the pet as part of the family; however, culturally, this is more of the exception and not the rule. A high percentage of black pet owners will not allow their pets to eat from their plates or lick their faces or sleep in their beds; and that's okay. There should be no pressure to love dogs, own dogs, or treat them like humans. As long as we don't treat them like 'dogs' we're in compliance with what's generally accepted by the majority. Personally, I have no interest in owning a dog or hanging around pets of any type; it's my prerogative. Equally, I have no interest in hating dogs or other pets, nor am I promoting such behavior. I also would never place greater value on any animal above a human being. I believe we should put greater energy into understanding the impact American history has had on black people, and ways to counter negativity. Again, we're more likely to show the dead body of a human on video than the carcass of a dead dog; one appears to be more acceptable and less appalling than the other; this type of desensitization can be dangerous. We shouldn't be in a rush to love animals over humans, there should be a sense of urgency to love people, all people. If you know a black person that's afraid of or have no interest in dogs, accept the fact that, generally speaking, we don't possess the inherent love for animals as pets as some other cultures, due in part to historical experiences. Give us time, this whole domesticating of the friendly family dog is still new to us. I also believe that if we choose to have dogs in our households, we should make great efforts to train and socialize the dogs. In most cases, dogs who have attacked people have been mistreated, malnourished, under socialized or a combination of these things. Increasing awareness of pet owners to what triggers dog misbehavior is a good place to start. Having affordable programs available for pet training and pet do's and don'ts will help to protect our families and communities from dog attacks and fatalities. Having dogs around to protect the house while the adults are away can be a wonderful thing when the dog can be trusted around the children.

Chapter Three

Who Doesn't Love Water?

Who Doesn't Love Water?

One of first things I heard growing up when it came to bodies of water was to go nowhere near it! My mother would stress this directive over and over, because there was story after story of a young black boy drowning in a lake, creek or swimming pool during those times. She didn't have to tell me twice, that was until I turned ten and decided I'd put my fears to the test. I remember jumping into a pool at a local YMCA not realizing I was on the deep end. Of course I didn't know how to swim and began sinking to the bottom quickly. As I fought and screamed while swallowing water, my heroic nephew, who was a couple years older than me, (I know, an older nephew, really? That's just how it was), jumped in and pulled me out; yes, he was black and knew how to swim. Years later I became a proficient swimmer more so for my kids' sake and to a lesser degree for recreation.

As I grew older I began to wonder, why is it that black people seem to be leery of bodies of water and the idea of swimming. We seem to enjoy pool parties and cruises; however, we can't swim and are afraid of large bodies of water; generally speaking, of course. Studies show that blacks rarely participate in water sports, learn to swim at much later ages than our white counterparts and prefer to shore fish over fishing in the middle of the lake. Although there have been great black swimmers, surfers, and water sportsmen/women, we seem to care very little about activities involving water. As is my recommendation whenever one seeks to understand the 'why' and the solution, let's take a brief look at the past.

Interestingly enough, one of the first uses of the term "Underground Railroad" is attributed to a slave master trying to catch his runaway slave. Tice Davids, a former slave, was running for freedom and had to swim across the Ohio River in 1831. Even though in a boat, the slave master couldn't catch him. He was quoted as saying, "He must have gone off on an underground railroad." Mr. Davids had actually survived the swim and resided in Ripley, Ohio. This quote was said, and is still debated, to prompt the naming of the system that helped runaway slaves. Many slaves risk and lost their lives in the Ohio river and other bodies of water attempting to escape bondage. Historically, Africans captured as slaves were excellent swimmers and divers. After being observed by European explorers, the decision was made to use a group of Africans to help with recovering sunken treasure form the Caribbean Sea. They were also used to extract pearls from the bottom of the sea. These were lucrative businesses; later, the business of building infrastructure in the new world took precedence.

Who could argue that American slave traders picked-up West Africans and loaded them onto overly crowded slave ships? Who could argue that the slavers filled these ships with human beings well beyond capacity, subsequently staking them like boxes one on top of one another? Who could argue that not every person piled on these ships survived the tenuous journey from West Africa through the middle passage and North America? No matter the gender of the would be slaves, no matter the status the West Africans may have held prior to being captured, no matter the place in which they were sold the one thing they all feared besides the evil slave traders and the idea of captivity, was new threat of water.

So as the slaves were piled on these ships they had no access to any facilities by which to relieve themselves. They of course were left to defecate and urinate on each other while chained and caged. Naturally people would become ill with fevers and all kinds of deceases as a result of this inhumane experience. Since slaves were nothing but cargo, (overstocked mind you), to these slavers they were expendable even if they were stacked together and on top of siblings, children and parents; imagine a mother forced to relieve herself on her child. Once a slave showed signs of illness of any kind he or she was brought on deck and flippantly tossed into sea as if they never existed; soulless animals. So the price for being sick was death, death by drowning in the ocean. Even if one had a simple cold or allergic reaction, the consequence was death. I wonder how many slaves hid their illnesses out of fear of death. Nonetheless, this practice of throwing slaves overboard was consistent, normal and anticipated. This was the main reason the ships were packed well beyond capacity.

Let's recognize the trauma echo that resulted from this. Because of the experiences of slaves on those ships and the reality that water was hell, an evil dark place no one wanted to be thrown into, many stories were told about the dangers of water. If you witnessed your loved ones thrown into water for being a little sick, maybe a headache or stomach virus was their crime punishable by death, how would you cope? What warnings would you share with others about bodies of water? Then what would you have shared when you realized that a body of water (the Ohio River) was the main path that stood between you and freedom?

The abolishment of slavery in 1868 was followed by Jim Crow laws which purpose was to offer undeniable evidence that African-Americans were required to regard themselves as second-class citizens. Some would say this separate-and-unequal law was America's Apartheid (laws that notoriously segregated South Africa from the late 1940's to early 1990's). Jim Crow laws protected racial prejudices and insulated racist law makers, law enforcement officers, business owners and educators from accountability and moral responsibility. Interracial marriage was prohibited, public accommodations had separate entrances for blacks and whites such as movie theaters; blacks had to sit on the balcony and were not allowed to have any contact with white patrons. Although the Thirteenth Amendment formally prohibited slavery, there was no amendment to stop or even encumber segregation; I believe some leaned on the first amendment to sooth their racism and bigotry.

In an effort to escape the tyranny of Jim Crow laws (more prevalent in the south), many African-Americans migrated to the north between 1890 and 1910. Although there were similar migrations to the west prior, the Great Migration to the north was more significant in terms of numbers, as it led to a second even larger migration from 1941 to 1970. As African-Americans were arriving in droves in northern cities, urban communities were being overturned and rapidly transitioning from predominately middle-class white communities to poor black over-populated urban centers. During this transition period segregation was alive and well and illuminated as more blacks migrated from the south.

When it came to access to public pools throughout the country, blacks were not allowed to enter bodies of water enjoyed by their white counterparts. This was both the letter and spirit of the law no matter the public or private space. We could not access beaches, recreation centers, hotel common areas, and of course we had no access to yacht and country clubs unless we were cooks or housekeepers. Consequently, we could not receive swim lessons legally or have trained lifeguards present if we wanted to be in or near water safely. Unfortunately, when swimming recreationally, black children are dying because of a lack of training and lifeguard supervision. According to the US Center for Disease Control, in a study from 2005-2009, the rate of fatal unintentional drowning for African American children is significantly higher than white children. African American deaths in swimming pools, for children ages 5-19, is almost 5.5 times higher than white children of the same age.

Most pools, particularly in the north, were in urban areas. Naturally, as blacks migrated north they wanted to swim and just enjoy beaches and water in general, as perceptions of bodies of water were beginning to change. However, this desire to enjoy water was not met with acceptance by whites. Their unwillingness was of course protected by Jim Crow and Civil Rights disparities. When white families began migrating from urban communities to the suburbs, also known as 'white-flight', they left the pools without water and/or the resources to maintain them. So the idea of blacks embracing swimming and water activities as culture was deferred. It wasn't until the late sixties that pools were legally desegregated. So to expect African-Americans to jump into, (pun intended), aquatic activities and aspire to be world-class swimmers is something that requires grandiose vision. That said; American history does include incredible black swimmers and swim teams that not only beat the odds, they dominate their sport.

I found that from 1952-1975 there were very few accounts of African American swimmers. Andrew Young had a swimming scholarship at Howard University from 1952-1956. Nate Clark was the first African American swimmer to score in an NCAA final at Ohio State in 1962 in the 200 yd. butterfly. It wasn't until 1988 that Sybil Smith, an African American female, scored in an NCAA event. With Anthony Erwin winning a gold and silver medal in the 2000 Olympics and Cullen Jones medaling gold in the 2008 Olympics, African Americans were and still challenging the stereotypes for not being good swimmers. In 2015 three African American swimmers finished one-two-three at the Women's Division I NCAA Championship in the 100yd freestyle. Simone Manuel set a new record in the event. Her teammate from Stanford, Lia Neal came in second, and finishing third was Natalie Hinds from the University of Florida. Hinds set her school's record in this event.

Even when we take a look at how water was used to strike down black people during the Civil Rights Movement, its obvious something as natural and pure as water was turned into a weapon to intimidate us. For some, stereotypes of African-Americans are a source of amusement and entertainment and often a good excuse to marginalize and discriminate against black people. Ignorance is the greatest threat against evolution and peace. When I hear people jokingly or seriously saying black people can't swim, I chuckle with tears. Chuckle because black people can swim; I'm one of them. Many black families raise their children around bodies of water and emphasize the importance of knowing how to swim if no other reason, to survive long enough to be rescued from a water hazard. I tear-up because I understand the history of blacks and bodies of water since the day we were introduced to America. We've only been allowed to legally learn how to swim and share bodies of water with our white brothers and sisters for fifty-years.

I would ask that we not only work harder to create, facilitate and fund aquatic programs for African-American children, we should work even harder to create, facilitate and fund pathways to understanding American History and aggressively moving toward sustainable change; not emotional or momentary action. Change doesn't happen by accident, it requires intentionality and metric-based outcomes over and over, and again. There are 633 United States colleges and universities that sponsor varsity swimming and diving team. This translates to schools being able to offer an average of 10 scholarships per year. Doing the math that is approximately 6000 full scholarships available per graduation year, or 12,000-18,000 partial scholarships available to each class. Having quality, affordable swimming programs for young African American children could open up doors for a college education that many students would not imagine walking through without exposure. We have to be intentional. We have to open doors for young people that have been closed for too long. Dispelling the trauma echoes associated with bodies of water that have been passed down through generations is critical to improving culture, and more importantly, to saving of lives.

Chapter Four

Rights to the Church

Rights to the Church

I believe hope is a basic need of all humans. Though hope isn't the most popular topic of many of our conversations, it is often the thing we reach for in times of struggle. When tragedy strikes many of us cry to God hoping for a miracle and comfort. Hope can be found in many ways and there has probably been excellent scholarly research done on how one may find hope. Men and women have probably traveled thousands of miles to find hope and the meaning thereof, but I know of a place right around the corner, where hope can be found; the local church. The right church can be a marvelous institution of learning and guidance. Their insight should be God-intended, God-inspired, and God-directed. It is indeed a precious gift of abundant good for wholeness of people who find their way to its sanctuary.

The black church was in full operation during slavery. Because blacks were not allowed to "learn" how to read, their knowledge of scripture was kept secret; however, they were able to communicate through signals and passwords that were not discernable by whites. They were able to share their faith with each other despite this "limitation." Over the years the black church evolved until it became a legitimate institution. Struggle has been the mantra of the black Christian for many years; this remains true today.

Many black Christians in America are challenged to love and respect a "Christian System" dominated by whites that excludes its influence and participation. Within the urban community, many feel as if the church has left them for greener pastures in the suburbs (where whites live). In many cases, the churches that are still situated in urban areas have congregations that are made up of people who commute from the suburbs. Many of the potential members feel left out and confused. They feel as if the church courted them only to leave them churchless, and that the local church does not identify with them or their circumstances; there is no connection. This puts the black church in a challenging predicament. The white church or the masses, considers us to be inferior and less qualified to teach or lead, and the black community thinks we believe that we are too good for them and completely out of touch. The historical black church has been a place where blacks could come to find peace and encouragement during unstable times of social and political unrest. Blacks could not only communicate with other blacks (friends, family members, etc.), they may not have seen in a long time but also share similar stories about struggling in a society that physically, emotionally and mentally oppressed them. The church provided a culture and an identity that was created for this particular population.

In his article, 'Is Multi-culturalism a threat to historically Black Churches', Douglas Ruffle mentions the historical significance of the church of addressing social and political unrest: "The agenda of African American churches has been mandated not only by the gospel and by institutional considerations, but also by the historical situation of their members. Slavery, oppression, institutional racism has been the context of that situation." In addition, the article presents an emerging trend in religious practice known as Afrocentric evangelical (led by Rev. Gerald Durley, pastor of Providence Missionary Baptist Church, Atlanta, Georgia) that is becoming popular in mainstream America. Jan Jarboe Russell in the article "The Man Who Saved Jane" in Talk magazine, describes Afrocentric evangelical as "combining evangelical theology with a proactive approach to spirituality and social activism in a way that affirms rather than chastises which attracts whites and blacks."

Ruffle makes a distinction in how the historic black church and some current church offspring were/are "judgmental and mean spirited" and how the previously mentioned United Methodist Churches are not harsh and critical. Although it may not be acceptable for a church to be judgmental and mean-spirited, the article does not mention what may have caused the churches to act in such a way. The historic black church was a place where blacks, both pastor and members could express anger at the inhumane and sinful treatment experienced by them. There is a difference between expressing anger that is a result of ungodly behavior and possessing a self-righteous attitude that the black church is the closest and perfect representative for God and everybody else does not achieve that standard. Blacks could attend church and receive the spiritual guidance and strength to endure the constant inhumane treatment for their existence – this was part of the historic black church identity.

In the book 'Operation Rebirth The Book: Black Church History Comes out of the Closet', Herndon L. Davis presents the case that historically Blacks and recently Gay and Lesbian men and women experienced oppression in the church although these groups participated in many of the same church practices as the White and heterosexual members respectively. The church oppressed them by "telling them they didn't matter and were not given a say in church matters that counted the most because of who they were". As a result, both groups were forced to separate and form other churches that could "specifically minister to their needs, experiences and culture".

Although the separation that occurred with both groups to start a movement for acceptance is similar, there may be specific differences experienced by the groups that caused the split. The book does not specifically mention the needs of each group therefore it is impossible to determine whether these needs are supposed to be addressed by the church institution. The time period wherein the separations occurred also is major in determining the causes of the split. The book does not mention the impact that the historic time period may have had on the causes of the church separation. The historic time period mentioned in the article is during the 1700s. Prejudice, discrimination, and oppression of blacks were quite visible, harmful, common and primarily accepted as a way of life by many Americans. Although not acceptable, at that time, the mainstream church existed in this painful culture; therefore, it is highly likely that the church assumed some of those unattractive qualities at least to some degree. Although currently in America some of those qualities may exist, the attributes are definitely not at the same brutal and blatant level as was the case in the 1700s. Therefore, the Black Gay/Lesbian men/women separation for the mainstream Black church occurring during the recent time period may be caused by different reasons.

The needs of the American society are currently different than the needs in the past. Historically church attendance and membership was mainly based on tradition and obligation and now church attendance and membership is predominantly based on a need to express deeply felt spiritual needs. Although the needs may be different on an individual level, but in general, today many church members will say that they attend church because they have been "raised in the church" or attended church regularly in their past as well as having a need for spiritual guidance. If tradition and obligation bring individuals to church where they receive what they need it is the church's responsibility to provide guidance and support. The church is intended for and should be accessible to all people, no matter their background; much like a hospital.

Every Christian Church should be open to all people as a place of love, acceptance and affirmation. All who desire to do so should be permitted to learn, grow and participate with only a few 'deal-breakers'. Those deal breakers do not include, but are not limited to, gender, race, age, pedigree, influence, economic condition, looks, docile-nature, friends or prestige. Unfortunately, the church and many of its leaders have become 'mini-gods' in their own minds and practices, as if they have every answer to all things and have an inside track on the voice of God and no one else can offer any meaningful insight or direction. This was not the intent of Jesus Christ, to make a mortal into a deity to rule over us. But somehow we've fallen into this belief that a human's word is absolute, final and non-negotiable on the merits of his or her title and appearance of holiness; this is unbiblical and unacceptable.

Although this is true amongst churches of all types, it's been my experience within black-led churches/ministries that an entire generation has been left out and being kept out due to the need for power and control and unchecked/unchallenged dominance amongst certain church leaders. Although they may have boards and committees, the Pastor has final authority when it comes to major decisions. In these cases, the idea of governance, referendums, and true biblical accountability is nothing more than a front to mislead parishioners. When you take a look at black churches (and churches in America in general) across this country, the one common denominator is that their numbers are shrinking. While there are churches that are experiencing phenomenal growth, the majority are going in the opposite direction. Sure this can be partially attributed to the incredible rise of the internet; however, the main cause, in my opinion, is poor interaction and the staunch judgmental nature of the church. Again, the church should be a place to go and find purpose and validation, instead it has become a place known for either wanting what's in your purse and condemnation. How could this happen you ask, by giving too much power to an individual or group and not realizing and tapping into the access and power of God through Jesus Christ directly, as individuals.

Results from a survey/study conducted by the Hartford Institute for Religion (HIRR) at Hartford Seminary. The survey found that churches grow by the following: 1) cultural affinity, finding "our kind of people"; 2) community involvement, keeping in touch; 3) organizational focus, vision in action; 4) offering both care and moral standards for members; and 5) finding inspiration in worship. Additionally, churches in suburbs are more likely to be growing, while those in rural areas are apt to be losing members. Four of the five reasons provided for church growth are directly related to church members. Actually the fourth reason is in part also related to church members but includes care provided by the pastor, elders, deacons or other church leadership. Besides the fourth reason, results did not include sermons/teachings/messages presented by the pastor as a major contributor to church growth.

The church has and will always be relevant within borders of the United States and throughout the world. The church, although many crimes against humanity have been committed in the name thereof, is intended and purposed to be a place of opportunity and acceptance with the intent to improve us all. As a black man, I don't know where I would be without the hope that Jesus Christ has given me. The obstacles I've faced due primarily to the color of my skin would have been impossible to overcome without my faith in God and his divine providence. My faith is the core of my essence and of my existence, and facilitator of my peace, provision and protection. While many share this faith, and many may not nor ever will, every person has a right to the option to know Jesus, access and serve the church.

Conclusion

Dogs, Water, Church and Black People ...sounds interesting, weird, funny, maybe even a little silly. How are these topics related? What is the purpose of even discussing them collectively? Historically speaking, dogs, water and even the church were all used in the process of subjugating black people under white authority. Blacks were not considered nor counted as being 100% human, therefore these mechanisms were critical to keeping us in our place in American society. Trauma echoes have perpetuated stereotypes that are not pushing our young people to rise to their potential nor challenge comfortable and accepted views about the African American community. The past has to exists in our conversations and be leveraged for a better future. How are we using the past? Are we using it to uplift and progress? Or are we using it as an excuse to tear down, regress or even stand still? Are we as a Nation in denial of our past? We can agree that black people are decades behind when it comes to domestic relationships with dogs. We can also agree that black people are generations behind when it comes to being competitive in water sports. However, we are not behind when it comes to going to church, but we are behind when it comes to the church coming to us.

It is my hope that this mini-book, (no matter the amount of endorsement or criticism), would start a larger and/or three distinct simultaneous conversations and provoke thought around these topics, inspire others to count on history (use it as advantage/leverage for a better future) instead of discounting it (running away from it), address and illuminate three dimensions of the African-American experience, and finally, promote and galvanize unity by understanding and appreciating our differences.

Bibliography

A Report on Religion in the United States Today. (2005). *Faith Communities Today.*

Addiction.com – (Trauma Echo), 2015
https://www.addiction.com/a-z/trauma-echo/

"College Swimming & Diving Scholarships Opportunities." N.p., n.d. Web. 14 Mar. 2016
www.scholarshipstats.com/swimming.html

 "Daily Archives: March 14, 2013." *The Sports Archives Blog.* N.p., n.d. Web. 14 Mar. 2016
http://www.thesportsarchivesblog.com/2013/03/14

Davis, H.L. (2005). Black Church history Comes Out of the Closet. *General Operation: Rebirth.*

"Here's A Map Of Where Your Pit Bull Isn't Welcome." *The Huffington Post.* N.p., n.d. Web. 14 Mar. 2016.
http://m.huffpost.com/us/entry/bsl-map_n_7216190.html

Ruffle, D. (2005). Is Multi-Culturalism a Threat to Historically Black Churches? *General Board of Global Ministries.*

"Safety Before Pit Bulldogs." *: Grippers in History.* N.p., n.d. Web. 24 Mar. 2016.
http://safetybeforebulldogs.blogspot.com/2015/12/grippers-in-history-19th-century-views.html?m=1

Stewart, C.F., (1994). African American Church Growth. Nashville: Abing Press.

"3 in 5 Americans Own Pets." MarketingCharts, N.p., 14 June 2011. Web. 14 Mar. 2016. http://www.marketingcharts.com/traditional/3-in-5-american-own-pets-17938/

"35 Dog Breeds That Have Attacked the Most People." *Dog Breeds That Have Attacked the Most People*. N.p., n.d. Web. 14 Mar. 2016. http://dogs.petbreeds.com/stories/4046/dog-breeds-attack#35-pit-bull

"Three College Swimmers Make History At NCAA Championship." *NBC News*. N.p., n.d. Web. 14 Mar. 2016. http://www.nbcnews.com/news/nbcblk/three-college-swimmers-make-history-ncaa-championship-n328906
"Tice Davids: The Runaway That Started." *Black Then*. N.p., 17 Apr. 2015. Web. 14 Mar. 2016. http://www.blackthen.com/tice-davids-the-runaway

"Top 10 Dogs For African Americans." *Elev8 RSS*. N.p., 29 July 2011. Web. 14 Mar. 2016. https://elev8.hellobeautiful.com/461005/top-10-dogs-for-african-americans-photos/

"2015 U.S. Dog Bite Fatalities - DogsBite.org." *DogsBite.org*. N.p., n.d. Web. 14 Mar. 2016. http://www.dogsbite.org/dog-bite-statistics-fatalities-2015.php

"Unintentional Drowning: Get the Facts." *Centers for Disease Control and Prevention*. Centers for Disease Control and Prevention, 24 Oct. 2014. Web. 14 Mar. 2016.
http://www.cdc.gov/HomeandRecreationalSafety/Water-Safety/waterinjuries-factsheet.html

"United States - Dog or Cat Ownership Rates by Race/ethnicity | Statistic 2011." *Statista*. N.p., n.d. Web. 14 Mar. 2016.
http://www.statista.com/statistics/250858/dog-or-cat-ownership-rates-of-us-households-by-race-ethnicity/

"U.S. Dog Bite Statistics - DogsBite.org." *DogsBite.org*. N.p., n.d. Web. 14 Mar. 2016.
http://www.dogsbite.org/dog-bite-statistics.php

About the Author

Kirk has been proudly married to his wife Venessa for over 25 years and they have three wonderful adult sons and one grandson. Their oldest and youngest sons are now serving in the United States Army, and their middle son is pursuing a degree in film and graphic design. Since 2002 Kirk has also served as Principle & CEO of Kirk Smith Unlimited & Associates, LLC., a company committed to help individuals, families and organizations become viable, impactful, visible, inspirational and deliverable holistically.

Kirk is a published author and op-ed columnist. He serves as an Adjunct Professor/Instructor for various Colleges and Universities. Specializing in leadership development, social justice, community engagement, marketing for nonprofits, organizational change, and public policy advocacy within both undergraduate and graduate studies programs.

Kirk was born and raised in Cincinnati, Ohio. He grew up in a single parent home, with 7 siblings in one of the largest most economically challenged communities in America. After graduating high school, Kirk served in the United States Army for seven years and is a wartime veteran.

Kirk has been a senior executive level operator of non-profit organizations and agencies, residential facilities, family centers, summer camps, community centers, community-based initiatives and social justice champion, as a President/CEO, District and Group Vice President, Senior Executive, and Director. He is also an ordained minister, and has been a motivational speaker and lecturer for over 20 years. Kirk holds a Bachelor of Science of Human Services and a Master of Science of Organizational Management and Leadership from Springfield College. He is a Doctoral Candidate (Ph.D.) in Human Services, specializing in Non-Profit Management & Leadership at Capella University. He is a nationally certified Nonprofit Organizational Leader & Leadership Development Professional.

Kirk has served on several boards supporting nonprofit community-based and higher education institutions. He has been featured on numerous national and local television shows and in news publications and magazines discussing community leadership development, education, fundraising, human and social service work in suburban, rural and urban communities and professional staff development. Kirk has been humbled by God's mercy, Jesus' power, and the Holy Spirit's presence. He's also been humbled by the love and patience of his wife and all the wonderful men and women who've given him opportunities. Kirk considers every aspect of his life as an opportunity to improve the lives of all those around him.

Kirk Ray Smith, BS, MS, ABD
kirksmithunlimited@gmail.org

Other Published Papers & Books (Links)

'Daily Insights of a Change Agent' (book)

http://www.amazon.com/Daily-Insights-Change-Agent-Insight/dp/1530785693/ref=sr_1_1?s=books&ie=UTF8&qid=1459617941&sr=1-1&keywords=daily+insights+of+a+change+agent

'The Business of a Non-Profit Organization'
Guest on Comcast News Makers Television Program

http://comcastnewsmakers.com/2014/10/10/kirk-smithpresident-and-ceo-ymca-of-greater-springfield/

Author of 'Call to the Cause Op-ed Series'
The Republican & Masslive Online News

http://blog.masslive.com/living_impact/print.html?entry=/2014/12/kirk_smith_never_underestimate_the_power_value_of_dreams.html

For booking, op-ed postings and video messages or additional information feel free to check out our website and social networks. We maintain an active presence on Twitter, Facebook, and YouTube.

www.ksmithunlimited.com
www.twitter.com/ksunlimited
www.facebook.com/kirksmithunlimited
www.youtube.com/kirksmithunlimited

Booking Contact Information

Marland McWilson, BS, MISM
Manager
marlandunlimited@gmail.com
813.597.1433

Jennifer Maceo Hernandez, BS, MS
Publicist
Jenniferunlimited@gmail.com
813.597-1433

Kirk Smith Unlimited